The Road To We

Premarital Couples Workbook

by
Jemece Gasaway, LMSW,
Monica Thompson, LPC, and
Latoyia R. Williams, MPA

The Road to We: Premarital Couples Workbook
published by Watersprings Publishing, a division of
Watersprings Media House, LLC.
P.O. BOX 1284
Olive Branch, MS 38654
www.waterspringsmedia.com
Contact publisher for bulk orders and permission requests.

Copyright © 2020 by Relationship Road Work, LLC., Jemece Gasaway, Monica Thompson, and Latoyia R. Williams

All rights reserved. No part of this publication may be reproduced, distributed, or transmitted in any form or by any means, including photocopying, recording, or other electronic or mechanical methods, without the prior written permission of the publisher, except in the case of brief quotations embodied in critical reviews and certain other noncommercial uses permitted by copyright law.

Printed in the United States of America.

ISBN-13: 978-1-948877-35-0

Thank you to our loving husbands and families who supported us through this journey and provided support and content for the material. Thank you God for our church, where we met, and for our church family who always gave us new perspectives.

Table of Contents

Welcome To Your Journey To Marriage 1

Week 1   Getting to Know Each Other 2

Week 2   Plotting Our Course 9

Week 3   Roles and Expectations 16

Week 4   Healing The Past 24

Week 5   Intimacy With God 28

Week 6   Boundaries 33

Week 7   Communication & Conflict 40

Week 8   Building Community 45

Week 9   Money Is A Tool 49

Week 10   Intimacy 56

Our Prayer for You 63

About the Authors 65

How to Use This Book

As you go through this workbook be sure that you both remain motivated to work through the lessons by progressing at a comfortable pace for both of you. The lessons will get harder and the questions will get tougher.

For each lesson, there will be homework. This homework is intended for you two to continue to dig and to connect on a deeper level. Grab a notebook to capture your thoughts and feelings as you go through the lessons.

The Road To We

Welcome To Your Journey To Marriage

For which one of you, when he wants to build a tower, does not first sit down and calculate the cost to see if he has enough to complete it?
Luke 14:28 NASB

How long do you plan to be married, 5-10 years? Most people would respond until one of us dies. The divorce rate shows that a high percentage of marriages don't last until death. If you responded until death, what are you doing to ensure that your future marriage lasts a lifetime? How many hours are you spending planning your wedding day compared to planning your married life? Again, what are you doing to ensure your future marriage lasts a lifetime? The Scripture above teaches us to count the cost of embarking on any endeavor. For you reading this book, the endeavor is marriage.

The **traditional wedding vows are** "*I, [name], take you [name], to be my [husband/wife], to have and to hold from this day forward,* **for better or for worse, for richer, for poorer, in sickness and in health, to love and to cherish**; *from this day forward until death do us part.*"

Thinking of these vows and your future wedding day, it is easy to imagine your future filled with many happy days and passionate sex-filled nights. You can quickly dream of happy times. Think about the phrase "for better." Where will you go on your honeymoon? Where will you go on your first anniversary trip? What will be your first major purchase as husband and wife? Think about the phrase "for worse." What does worse look like to you? Are you willing to change your eating habits because she wants to be whole food plant-based, a vegan? Next, think about the phrase "for richer, for poorer." Are you willing to sign a prenuptial agreement? How would poverty impact your dreams? What if your spouse cannot find consistent work for years? Next, think about the phrase, "in sickness and in health." How would you adjust to abstinence because the doctor warns against having sex until after she gives birth and she's only 4 months pregnant? Are you willing to care for him after a massive heart attack at age 32? Lastly, think about the phrase, "to love and to cherish." Has anyone ever loved or cherished you before, if so how does your future spouse compare? If your future spouse is the only person who has ever cherished you, does that make them the perfect person to marry?

As you spend time working through this workbook with your future spouse, you will begin to dig deep into your views on communication, conflict, finances, sex, roles and commitment and your view of marriage as a lifelong journey.

Let's get started on building a lifelong relationship!

WEEK 1
Getting To Know Each Other

Objectives
- Create a safe environment for connection
- Consider both of your expectations of working through this book

Advance Preparation
- None

Building Your Connection

When you marry, you make a vow to God and a promise to love your spouse regardless of what the future holds. You make a commitment to love your spouse on their worst days; to maintain your love when the relationship is no longer fun or thrilling; and to sacrificially love for the good of the other person. The measure of love God has for you, is the measure of love you should have for your spouse. One way to love your future spouse is to value their uniqueness.

By God's design, there are natural differences between men and women which cause you to think and react differently. Each of you were created by God and given your own talents, qualities, spiritual gifts, personalities, and character traits. The environment you grew up in, the experiences you had, your beliefs, personalities, and values lend to your individual shaping. Your future marriage will be a byproduct of your individuality. Just remember your differences are from God and should be valued.

Choosing to value each other daily by deciding to view your future spouse as a priceless gift from God will lead to emotional safety within your relationship. On the other hand, choosing not to value each other's differences can lead to problems ignited by comparison, judging, competition, and the frustration of unmet expectations.

In this week's lesson you will grow in your knowledge of each other, develop an appreciation of your differences, and increase your emotional connection.

Lesson Activities

This activity will allow you to get to know each other in a humorous way. Don't just pose the questions to each other, peel the onion and ask each other to explain the 'why' behind your answers.

Would you rather questions[1]

- Would you rather find your true love or a suitcase with five million dollars inside?
- Would you rather be able to see 10 minutes into your own future or 10 minutes into the future of anyone but yourself?
- Would you rather be married to a 10 with a bad personality or to a 6 with an amazing personality?
- Would you rather be famous when you are alive and forgotten when you die or unknown when you are alive and famous after you die?
- Would you rather go to jail for 4 years for something you didn't do or get away with something horrible you did and always live in fear of being caught?
- Would you rather live in the wilderness far from civilization or live on the streets of a city as a homeless person?
- Would you rather never use social media sites or apps again or never watch another movie or TV show?
- Would you rather have an easy job working for someone else or work for yourself and work incredibly hard?
- Would you rather be completely invisible for one day or be able to fly for one day?
- Would you rather live without the internet or live without A/C and heating?
- Would you rather have a horrible job and be able to retire comfortably in 10 years or have your dream job and have to work until the day you die?
- Would you rather be able to teleport anywhere or be able to read minds?
- Would you rather know when you are going to die or how you are going to die?

---

[1] "Would you Rather Questions," https://conversationstartersworld.com/would-you-rather-questions/

 ## Homework Based On This Week's Lesson

Use the Love Map list of questions on the following pages and spend 15-minutes 3 times a week, each week, talking about the questions and going deeper together in an effort to build a connection. Seclude yourselves from distractions and take your time going through the questions. Remember it isn't an interview to find out facts about each other; you are wanting to know the other person more deeply and understand the 'why' behind the facts. Guard against allowing these questions to result in a disagreement if one of you doesn't know as much as the other.

An Example Dialogue

- Person 1: Who are your two closest friends?
- Person 2: My two closest friends are Michelle and Rochelle.
- Person 1: *[Ask probing questions]* Why are they your closest friends? What do you like about both of them? How long have you been close? What do you have in common with both or either of them? When you hang out with them, what do you enjoy doing?

Homework In Preparation For The Next Lesson

- In preparation for the next lesson, complete the Relationship Check and Vision activity.

References

Gottman, John and Nan Silver: *The Seven Principles for Making Marriage Work: A Practical Guide From the Country's Foremost Relationship Expert*, (New York: Three Rivers Press, 1999).

"Relationship Vision," https://cornercanyoncounseling.com/wp-content/uploads/2015/05/Your-Relationship-Vision.pdf

"Would you Rather Questions," https://conversationstartersworld.com/would-you-rather-questions/

Love Map Questions[2]

1. Who are your two closest friends?
2. What is your favorite musical group, composer, or instrument?
3. What is one of your hobbies?
4. What stressors are you facing right now?
5. Describe in detail what you did today or yesterday.
6. What is the date of your dating anniversary?
7. Who is your favorite relative?
8. What is your favorite flower?
9. What is one of your greatest fears or disaster scenarios?
10. What is your favorite time of day?
11. What makes you feel most complete?
12. What is your favorite meal?
13. What is your favorite way to spend the evening?
14. What is your favorite color?
15. What personal improvements do you want to make in your life?
16. What kind of present would you like best?
17. What was one of your best childhood experiences?
18. What was your favorite vacation?
19. What is one of your favorite ways to be soothed?
20. Who is your greatest source of support (other than me)?
21. What is your favorite sport?
22. What do you most like to do with time off?
23. What is one of your favorite weekend activities?
24. What is your favorite getaway place?
25. What is your favorite movie?

---

[2] All questions adapted from Gottman, John and Nan Silver: *The Seven Principles for Making Marriage Work: A Practical Guide From the Country's Foremost Relationship Expert* (New York: Three Rivers Press, 1999).

Premarital Couples Workbook

26. What are some of the important events coming up in your life? How do you feel about them?
27. What are some of your favorite ways to work out?
28. Who was your best friend in childhood?
29. What is one of your favorite magazines?
30. Name one of your major rivals or "enemies."
31. What would you consider your dream job?
32. What do you fear the most?
33. Who is your least favorite relative?
34. What is your favorite holiday?
35. What kinds of books do you most like to read?
36. What is your favorite TV show?
37. What are you most sad about?
38. What medical problems do you worry about?
39. What was your most embarrassing moment?
40. What was your worst childhood experience?
41. Name two of the people you admire most.
42. Of all the people we both know, who do you like the least?
43. What is one of your favorite desserts?
44. Name one of your favorite novels?
45. What are two of your aspirations, hopes, or wishes?
46. Do you have a secret ambition? What is it?
47. Which foods do you hate?
48. What is your favorite animal?
49. What is your favorite song?
50. Which sports team is your favorite?

Relationship Check & Vision[3]

In this activity, each of you will identify characteristics of a satisfying love relationship.

1. Take out two sheets of paper, one for each of you. Working separately write a series of short sentences that describe your personal vision of a deeply satisfying love relationship. Include qualities you already have that you want to keep and qualities you wish you had. Write each sentence in the present tense, as if it is already happening. e.g. "We have fun together." Make all your items positive statements (i.e. "We settle differences peacefully" rather than "We don't fight")**
1. Share your sentences. Note the items that you have in common and underline them. (It doesn't matter if you have used different words, as long as the general meaning is the same.) If your partner has written sentences that you agree with but did not think of yourself, add them to your list. Ignore items that are not shared.
2. Now turn to your own expanded list and rank each sentence with a number from 1 to 5 according to its importance to you, with 1 indicating "very important" and 5 indicating "not so important", circle the two items that are most important to you.
3. Put a check mark beside those items that you think would be most difficult for the two of you to achieve.
4. Now work together to design a mutual relationship vision. Start with the items that you both agree are most important. Put a check mark by the items that you both agree would be difficult to achieve. If you have items that are a source of conflict between you, see if you can come up with a compromise statement that satisfies both of you. If not, leave the item off your combined list.

*If you cannot identify any characteristics of a satisfying relationship, identify displeasing characteristics. Then, reword those statements into positive statements. Try to focus on the positive.

---

[3] "Relationship Vision," https://cornercanyoncounseling.com/wp-content/uploads/2015/05/Your-Relationship-Vision.pdf

Premarital Couples Workbook

Characteristics of a Fulfilling Marriage

Materials

- 4 inch square wooden plaques (alternatively, use a ½ sheet of paper)
- Fine tip or medium tip markers

Lesson Activity

As a couple, you will create a plaque. This can be used as an ornament or a decorative element in your new home. Think of the attributes of the ideal marriage and write them on the plaque. Below is an example of a completed plaque. **Note**: If you use wood, you will have to treat the wood to accept the marker ink.

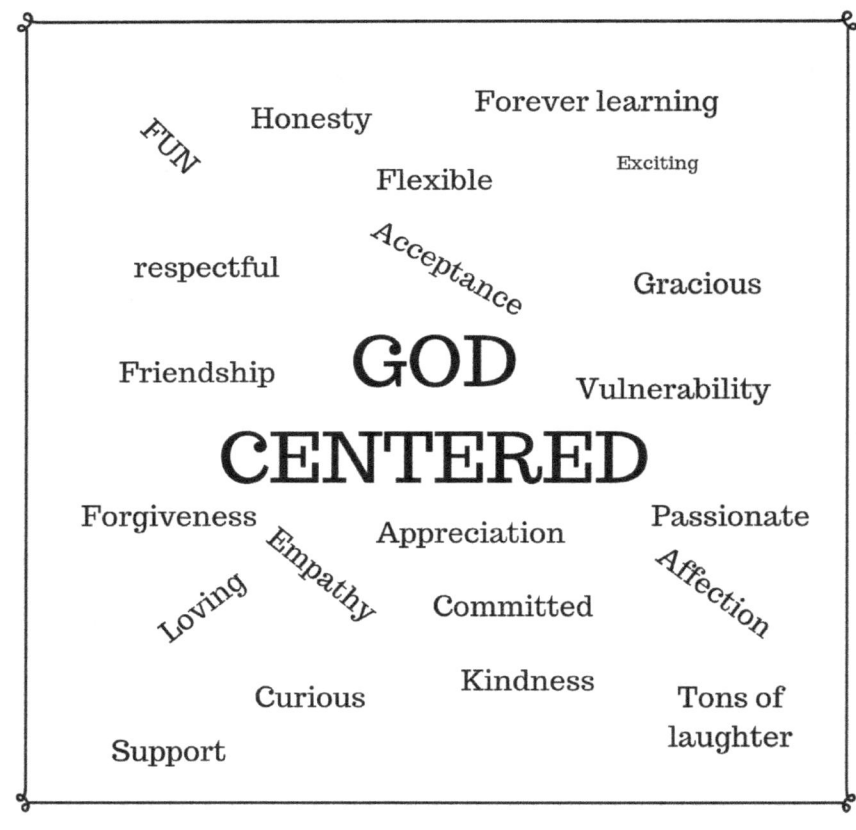

WEEK 2

Plotting Our Course

Objectives

- Consider God's design for your life as an individual and a future married couple
- Discuss the benefits and sacrifices of living according to God's will and purpose
- Develop a roadmap for marriage

Materials

- Bible or Bible app
- Magazines
- Glue sticks
- Scissors
- Markers and Pens
- Poster boards OR butcher paper/roll
- Your Relationship Check & Vision homework

Advance Preparation

- The completed Relationship Check and Vision homework from the previous week.

Building Your Connection

It is said that adults, on average, make at least 35,000 decisions each day. These daily decisions range from minor, to important, to life altering. Many are quick and made without much thought or consideration, while some decisions are more weighted, and others are often agonized over. One of the most important decisions you'll ever make is whom to marry, so consider the decision strongly. Scripture offers guidance about issues we face. When looking to God's word for decision making guidance, it is easy to identify those commands which are concretely written, but it can be more difficult when things aren't as concrete. What should we do when the Bible doesn't speak directly to the situations we face and the decisions we need to make? Decision making can be tough for an individual and even tougher for a couple pursuing harmony and collaboration. Therefore, it is very important that you and your future spouse have a decision making process in place for times of disparity; one is included later in this chapter. Use the Decision Making Model / Conflict Resolution Model to discuss a single topic and to drive to a solution.

Lesson Activities

Open in prayer and discuss these questions with each other about the homework to talk 15-minutes 3 times a week.

- How difficult has it been to spend 15 minutes talking 3 times a week?
- What did you learn about your significant other or yourself while doing the homework?
- What surprised you about the exercise?
- How will you work towards incorporating this activity into the rhythm of your relationship?

This week's lesson will begin by focusing on God's design for individuals and couples. With an understanding of God's design, you will develop a marriage roadmap. This week's activities will facilitate open communication and will provide you insight into the expectations you have of each other and your future. Be creative and have fun!

Scripture

Read and discuss the following Scriptures on singleness, marriage, and goal setting.

Singleness

Read Genesis 2:18 and Genesis 2:21–24.

- What are some advantages and disadvantages of being alone?
- How comfortable are you being alone?
- What are the characteristics of a helper?

Marriage

Read 1 Corinthians 16:13–14, Romans 12:9–13, and Matthew 19:5–6.

- How do you demonstrate humility and gentleness in your relationship?
- What does commitment look like in your current relationship?
- What does honor look like in your current relationship?
- Have there been people who have tried to separate you and your future spouse? What were the reasons given, if any? Can you understand their reasons for encouraging you to separate?
- What is one truth you can take away from the message of the person trying to separate you?
- How do you plan to keep people from separating you and your future spouse?

Goal Setting

Read Psalms 127:1–2, Proverbs 16:8–9, Proverbs 21:4–6, and Proverbs 19:20-21.

- Why did God create you specifically? What is your purpose?
- What are the benefits to living according to God's will for your life?
- What are some of the sacrifices you may have to make?
- Which of those sacrifices are you willing to make?
- Why are you struggling to make other sacrifices?

Premarital Couples Workbook

Your Roadmap

Review the results of your Relationship Vision activity. Discuss some of the values that will guide your future marriage.

An Example
- We will pray together daily.
- We will respect each other.
- We will seek God before complaining to the other person about hurt feelings.
- We will look out for each other's best interest.
- We will make each other better and strive for more.
- We will realize what we can lose.
- We will take timeouts for a maximum of 2 hours when needed.
- We will serve our local church regularly.
- We will support our local church financially.
- We will volunteer in the community monthly.
- We will be part of a community of committed married couples.

Using your Relationship Vision, magazines, glue sticks, scissors, and poster boards or butcher block paper, you will create your own marriage roadmap. The marriage roadmap will be used and referenced throughout this workbook as a guide and a basis for decision making. Remember to make changes to the marriage roadmap as needed. There is a roadmap example on the pages that follow.

Areas to consider:

Financial	Spiritual	Relational	Familial / Children
Health	Professional	Self-improvement	Social
Community	Hobbies		

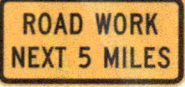 **Homework Based On This Week's Lesson**

- Complete the Marriage Roadmap.
- Continue working through the Love Map questions until completed and spend 15-minutes talking 3 times a week.

Homework In Preparation For The Next Lesson

- Begin a new habit of planning for the upcoming week. This activity will help you anticipate each other's needs and possibly be more gracious with minor offenses. Ask each other:
    - What events are you looking forward to this week?
    - What events are you dreading?
    - What will a successful week look like for you?
- Identify at least 10 expectations you have of yourself and 10 expectations you have of your future spouse. Some examples include cooking every day, having sex 7 days a week, being a stay-at-home mom, spending holidays at my family's home, washing the cars, etc.

References

Norman Cotterell, PhD, "The Relationship Vision," Beck Cognitive Behavioral Therapy, https://beckinstitute.org/the-relationship-vision/

Premarital Couples Workbook

Marriage Roadmap Example

Sept 2020:
Wedding Day

Sept 2020:
Honeymoon

Oct 2020:
Join a church

Nov 2020:
Jerry gets a new job

Jan 2021: Lynn quits her job and returns to school

Mar 2021: Pay off 25% of Jerry's student loans

Jan 2023:
Vacation

Dec 2022:
Pay off 25% of Jerry's student loans

July 2022:
Lynn gets a new job

June 2022:
Pay off 25% of Jerry's student loans

Dec 2021:
Buy Lynn a new car

Mar 2023: Pay off Jerry's student loans

June 2023:
Buy a house

May 2023:
Have first baby

Nov 2025:
Buy Jerry a new car

Mar 2025:
Family vacation

Dec 2024:
Jerry gets a new job

May 2024:
Daughter graduates

Dec 2041:
Son graduates

Nov 2028:
Mission Trip

May 2026:
Begin saving for college

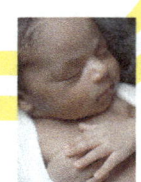
May 2026:
Have second baby

Decision Making and Conflict Resolution Model

What is the topic to be discussed?	
His Response	Her Response

What is a good time and place to discuss the topic?	
His Response	Her Response

How do you and your future spouse view the topic?	
His Response	Her Response

How have you and your future spouse tried to address the topic in the past?	
His Response	Her Response

What are 10 possible solutions? REQUIRED!!			
1.		6.	
2.		7.	
3.		8.	
4.		9.	
5.		10.	

How will each of you work towards executing the selected decision?	
His Response	Her Response

What is a good time and place to meet to evaluate our progress?	
His Response	Her Response

Premarital Couples Workbook

WEEK 3

Roles and Expectations

Objectives
- Evaluate your opinion of reasonable and unreasonable expectations
- Consider the roles and expectations God has for husbands and wives

Materials
- Bible or Bible app
- Pens
- Reasonable and Unreasonable Questions
- The 5 Love Languages Quiz link, https://www.5lovelanguages.com/profile/
- DISC Assessment link, https://openpsychometrics.org/tests/ODAT/

Advance Preparation
- Complete the 5 Love Languages Quiz, the DISC assessment, and the Accepting Influence Quiz (available on paper only), and discuss the results with your future spouse. **Note**: If you have recently completed any personality assessment, then skip the DISC assessment.

Building Your Connection

If someone told you that marriage was 50/50 and that's what you expect, you are set up to be disappointed. There is no such thing as a 50/50 marriage. There are seasons that will change your ability to contribute to the relationship and the family. Single parent, women-led households are more the norm than the exception and when women marry they usually aren't getting married with the idea that they're *just* going to be a 'helper suitable for him'. The impact of fatherless homes has many women brought up today with the attitude that they are good on their own. This attitude is brought into their romantic relationships; often times before the relationship has a chance to develop. As you work through this lesson, don't strive for equality, instead focus on what will work best for the two of you as you become **ONE**.

Countless sermons, books, blogs, magazine articles have been written about Biblical Roles of a Husband or a Wife. We aren't going to add anything new and different to those other sources. We encourage you to review those old sermons, articles, or books before you marry and discuss them with your significant other.

Lesson Activities

This week's lesson will focus on God's expectations of individuals and couples, the roles of men and women, and expectations in marriage. This week's activities will help you establish rules within your future family and increase your ability to communicate your needs. Open in prayer and discuss these questions with each other:

- How does the roadmap support the Relationship Vision we created as a homework assignment in the previous lesson?
- Is the marriage roadmap skewed towards the goals of one person?
- How will we be stretched to achieve the goals on your marriage roadmap?
- How does the marriage roadmap allow us to use our strengths and illuminate our weaknesses?
- If as a couple you complete every goal on your marriage roadmap, when you close your eyes for the last time, will you be pleased with your life? Will God be pleased?

Scriptures

Review and discuss Scriptures on God's expectations of individuals and couples.

Headship and Submission
- Discussing this topic may be challenging for you because the term submission has many negative connotations. **Mark 12:30–31** commands us to love God and to love our neighbors as we love ourselves. We define submission as obeying the command to love God and our neighbor, who is our significant other and future spouse in this instance. **Note**: Find a spiritually mature person to help facilitate this discussion if needed.
- ***Read Ephesians 5:21-30, 1 Corinthians 11:3, and Col 3:18-19***.

Below are questions to ask each other:
- What does submission mean according to the Bible?
- What are some ways the biblical term submission is abused?
- What are some of the horror stories you've heard about submission?
- What are some correct applications of the biblical term submission?
- What is reasonable submission according to these Scriptures?
- What is unreasonable submission according to these Scriptures?
- Ask yourself, what if your future husband is not a leader? Who leads?
- Ask yourself, am I marrying them because they agree to do everything I want?

Review the assessments completed in preparation for this lesson and discuss the questions below together.

5 Love Languages
- What are ways your significant other can express love to you in your preferred love language?
- What did you learn about your significant other?

DISC
- In your opinion, how accurate was your assessment?
- What are some behaviors that you may need to modify as you begin to build a life

with your significant other?
  - For example, awareness of your tone, the ability to problem solve, the ability to communicate both feelings and facts, or the ability to resolve conflicts in a healthy manner.

Accepting Influence

This assessment is on the following pages. Complete the assessment and discuss the results together.

- What did you learn about yourself?

Roles & Responsibilities

As you're discussing roles and responsibilities, ask each other:

- Describe the way your job would function if no one was in charge.
- What is the impact to your relationship if no one leads?
- What is the impact to your relationship if both of you try to lead?
- Describe your home life if you or your future spouse did whatever either of you wanted without regard for the other person. What problems would emerge?
- How did you see the role of the husband and the role of the wife modeled in your home growing up?
- How did you see the roles modeled by others in your community growing up?
- How have your observations of the two roles from childhood influenced your view of your future role as a husband or as a wife?
- If you haven't seen healthy examples of your future role, how will you learn to fulfill your role?

The key to these questions is to highlight healthy and unhealthy behaviors observed and to bring awareness to the need for healthy role models as husbands and wives. Most people know what they don't want to be or what they don't want to do as a husband or a wife, but fewer people know how to be the husband or wife they want to be.

- What do you think are reasonable expectations?
- What do you think are unreasonable expectations?
- How will you respond if your expectations go unmet?
- What are the responsibilities you and your future spouse have decided on that you disagree with?
- Reviewing the homework from the previous lesson, do you still have the same expectations of yourself?
- Reviewing the homework from the previous lesson, do you still have the same expectations of your future spouse?

Expectations Game

Play the Expectations Game with your significant other. Ask each other the Reasonable vs. Unreasonable list of questions and each person responds to the question. Discuss your differences in opinion.

The Road To We

Expectations Game - Reasonable vs. Unreasonable Questions

1. I expect to always be happy in my marriage.
2. I expect my spouse to be faithful to me.
3. I expect my spouse to know what I need.
4. I expect my spouse to be completely honest with me.
5. I expect my spouse to always agree with me.
6. I expect my spouse to trust me.
7. I expect my spouse to care about health as much as I do.
8. I expect my spouse to express concern about the connection in our relationship.
9. I expect my spouse to accept my same-sex friends.
10. I expect to be an equal partner with my spouse in our relationship.
11. I expect my spouse to accept my opposite sex friends.
12. I expect my spouse never to hit me.
13. I expect we will not have to work to make our marriage work.
14. I expect my spouse to keep a clean house.
15. I expect my spouse to enjoy the activities I enjoy.
16. I expect my spouse to talk to me about any challenges in our relationship.
17. I expect my spouse to want sex as often as I do.
18. I expect my spouse to handle all household matters.
19. I expect my spouse to want to always want to spend time with me.
20. I expect my spouse to go to work as expected by their employer.
21. I expect my spouse to fill every one of my needs.
22. I expect my spouse to handle all financial matters.
23. I expect my spouse to make me happy when I'm sad or need cheering up.
24. I expect to have some time by myself when I need.
25. I expect my spouse to always dress to impress me.
26. I expect my spouse to value our differences.
27. I expect to be the center of my spouse's world.
28. I expect my spouse to show me affection in public as well as at home.
29. I expect my spouse to be my soulmate.
30. I expect my spouse to support any of my activities outside the home.

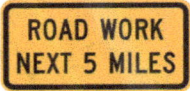 ## Homework Based On This Week's Lesson

- Continue setting aside 15-minutes, 3 times a week to talk and to complete any outstanding homework and prepare for the upcoming week.
- Find ways to exercise your future spouse's love language, excluding physical touch.

Homework In Preparation For The Next Lesson

- Each of you is to make a list of people who have hurt you (including yourself) and those you have not forgiven. Write each person's offense next to their name, including yourself, and explain why you haven't forgiven each person.

References

"DISC Assessment Test," Open-Source Psychometrics Project, https://openpsychometrics.org/tests/ODAT/

Gary Chapman, "The 5 Love Languages," *The 5 Love Languages*, https://www.5lovelanguages.com/profile/couples/

Gottman, John and Nan Silver: *The Seven Principles for Making Marriage Work: A Practical Guide From the Country's Foremost Relationship Expert* (New York: Three Rivers Press, 1999).

Accepting Influence Questionnaire[4]

Answer each statement true or false.

Question	True	False
I'm really interested in my partner's opinion on our basic issues.		
I usually learn a lot from my partner's opinion on our basic issues.		
I want my partner to feel that what he or she says really counts with me.		
I generally want my partner to feel influential in our relationship.		
I can listen to my partner but only up to a point.		
My partner has a lot of basic common sense.		
I try to communicate respect even during our disagreements.		
If I keep trying to convince my partner, I will eventually win out.		
I don't reject my partner's opinions out of hand.		
My partner is not rational enough to take seriously when we discuss our issues.		
I believe in lots of give and take in our discussion.		
I am very persuasive and usually can win arguments with my partner.		
I feel I have an important say when we make decisions.		
My partner usually has good ideas.		
My partner is basically a great help as a problem solver.		
I try to listen respectfully even when I disagree.		
My ideas for solutions are usually much better than my partners.		
I can usually find something to agree with in my partner's position.		
My partner is usually too emotional.		
I am the one who needs to make the major decisions in this relationship.		

---

[4] Gottman, John and Nan Silver: *The Seven Principles for Making Marriage Work: A Practical Guide From the Country's Foremost Relationship Expert* (New York: Three Rivers Press, 1999).

WEEK 4
Healing the Past

Objectives

- Identify potential causes of the feelings associated with sadness, pain, and anger
- Determine ways God can use these experiences for His glory
- Recognize the impact the past can have on the present and the behaviors produced by unresolved hurt
- Understand the role forgiveness plays in healing the pain from the past

Materials

- Bible or Bible app

Advance Preparation

- None

Building Your Connection

You have brought good and bad past experiences into your relationship and future marriage. When there is unforgiveness, it will bleed into your relationship and will impact your future marriage. Unresolved pain can result in you hurting each other. You want to start your marriage off with a solid foundation so begin the process of forgiveness, not necessarily for the sake of the person who has hurt you but for your own sake.

This week's lesson will develop your awareness of past events that have produced pain, sadness, or anger. After opening in prayer, check in with each other by asking questions differently or else checking in with each other will become uninteresting. Below are other questions to ask:

- How are we creating new habits of building love maps and knowing the highs and lows of each other's days and weeks?
- Different ways to ask the check-in questions:
  - What risks did you take today?
  - How did you fail today?
  - How did you exceed your expectations today?
  - How did you surprise yourself today?
  - What did you do today that would make God smile?

Lesson Activities

The activities in this week's lesson will engage you experientially in the process of self-awareness and healing. You will gain valuable insight into unexpressed pain and possible behavioral issues. With this information, you can determine if either of you needs to seek the services of a professional counselor.

Scriptures

Read through Scriptures related to forgiveness.
Read Colossians 3:12–14, Luke 17:3–4, and Ephesians 4:29–32.

Steps To Forgive

Share at least one example of unforgiveness with your significant other. Below are some questions to ask each other:

- How difficult was it to develop a list of people you haven't forgiven?
- How difficult was it to acknowledge the reasons you haven't forgiven them?
- What feelings did this activity bring up?
- Did you sit with the sadness, pain, or anger associated with the events or did you run from those feelings?
  - If you ran away from your feelings, how did you escape the feelings? (eat, drink,

shop, etc.)
- How do you normally deal with feelings you don't want to face head on?
- If you want to begin to forgive someone, these are some helpful steps:
  - Take time to think about the sadness, pain, or anger.
  - Pray for each other, the person whom you haven't forgiven, and any others who may have been hurt. Pray for healing in all of the impacted relationships.
  - Remember God forgave and commands forgiveness.
  - Think about a time when you hurt someone.
  - Find Scriptures to memorize related to forgiveness.

Impacts Of The Highs And Lows Of Your Life

During this activity, you may be exposed to memories of events and unsettling feelings. Discuss a happy event besides your engagement (high) and a sad event (low) in your childhood and adulthood.

Below are probing questions to ask each other:
- What is the impact of these events on your behaviors and decisions as an adult?
- What did you learn about relationships from these events?

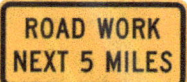 ## Homework Based On This Week's Lesson

- Develop a plan to begin your journey of letting go and forgiving the people on your list. Remember why God commands forgiveness and the impacts unforgiveness has on relationships. You'll want to find someone to hold you accountable for moving towards forgiveness.
- Continue setting aside 15-minutes, 3 times a week to talk and exercising the habit of preparing for the upcoming week.
- Continue updating your marriage roadmap.

Homework In Preparation For The Next Lesson

- Make a list of at least 7 things necessary to have an intimate relationship with God and complete the Spiritual Pathways Assessment, https://groupleaders.org/spiritual-pathways-assessment/

References

Gottman, John and Nan Silver: *The Seven Principles For Making Marriage Work: A Practical Guide From the Country's Foremost Relationship Expert* (New York: Three Rivers Press, 1999).

"Spiritual Pathways Assessment," Group Leaders, https://groupleaders.org/spiritual-pathways-assessment/

WEEK 5

Intimacy With God

Goals

- Define intimacy with God and the benefits
- Review practical examples of intimacy with God
- Recognize hindrances to a closer relationship with God
- Explore ways to routinely build an intimate relationship with God

Materials

- A Bible or Bible App, each person will need their own
- Spiritual Pathways Assessment

Advance Preparation

- None

Building Your Connection

Many people develop religious habits as a way of 'feeling' close to God. These habits include attending numerous church services or religious events in an attempt to make up for a hardened heart. Participation in these activities cannot replace true intimacy with God. Just like you cannot develop intimacy with your future spouse by talking to them once a month, you cannot develop true intimacy with God without talking and listening to Him.

Learning to be a spouse the way God intends, requires you learning God's way. Incorporate spending time in God's word and in prayer into your life. This will not guarantee that life will be perfect or easy but this practice will help prepare you for the challenges of life.

This week's lesson is about helping you grow in intimacy with God and developing a routine you can implement tomorrow. Begin this lesson by praying about your individual intimacy with God, your collective intimacy with God, for an open heart, and your upcoming marriage. After the opening prayer, asnwer these questions:

- What is keeping us from spending at least 15-minutes three times a week together?
  - If we don't have time now, when will we have time?
- What's something new you've learned about your significant other as you're spending time talking 3 times a week?
- What are other rituals you're trying to incorporate into your lives?

Lesson Activities

Develop a definition of intimacy with God. Based on your definition, below are some questions to ask:

- Why don't you strive for intimacy with God?
- What are you afraid of?
- How will drawing closer to God impact your conversations? Your relationship with your significant other? Television you watch? Music you listen to? Places you spend money? Ways you use money?

Review practical ways you can grow in intimacy with God. This activity will help take the mystery out of knowing how to grow in relationship with God.

- Identify your time of day. This time is best if it is unhurried time with God in prayer and His word.
- Prayer – There are a number of resources that can help you learn to pray.
  - Check out this website for quick highlights on prayer, https://www.desiringgod.org/articles/prayer-for-beginners
- Reading the Bible – Begin this week by reading the Book of James, a practical book. Over the next weeks and months, read the Book of Mark, a quick read about things Jesus did and then read the Book of John which focuses on what Jesus said. Remember to read slow enough to comprehend and to document any truths you may learn while reading.
- If you're willing, journal your prayers and answers to prayers so you can watch God

move through you life and the lives of others.

- Review online resources available to do more in depth Bible study:
  - https://www.preceptaustin.org/
  - https://www.focusonthefamily.com/faith/the-study-of-god/why-study-the-bible/why-study-the-bible
  - YouVersion's Bible app has some devotionals.
  - Cru.org and Intervarsity.org both have *well developed plans with videos to help any new believer begin their journey of growing in Christ*

Review the homework to complete the Spiritual Pathways Assessment. This is an assessment that identifies other ways in which people draw closer to God. These are not a substitute for time alone with God spent in His word or in prayer.

- What was the result of your Spiritual Pathways Assessment?
- How do you think you can exercise this method of drawing closer to God?

Briefly review expectations of yourself and God in growing in intimacy with God.

Self

- Intimacy is not just knowledge about God. Remember feeling distant from God is a matter of our sin, lack of trust, or disappointment with God, it doesn't reflect God's proximity.
- What are some ways you have fallen into the practice of religion?

Expectations of God

- What if you become a "good Christian" and pray, stop some sins, go to church most weekends, attend a few bible studies, give an offering, and life isn't free of troubles?

What then? Remember that…

- God is not a holy vending machine.
- Some prayers are not answered in our time.
- Some people do get sick and die at any age.
- Some answers to prayers are "no" without a reason given.
- Some marriages end.
- Some people don't change, no matter how much you cry out to God.
- Some people are laid off and go without jobs for a while.
- Some people have to move back in with their parents or in-laws.

The point to these statements is that God has not promised us a perfect life without hardship or disappointment.

Sample Bible Study

This is intended to be a quick demonstration of how to get started spending time with the Bible.

- Take turns reading through James 1:1–8 as a couple.
- Take turns reading the same verses using different translations (NASB, NIV, NKJV).
- Read a commentary on the verses. See the James commentaries at https://www.preceptaustin.org/bybook/59
- Finally, summarize what you read but don't make any applications. Highlight truths that you can take from the Scripture without reading into the Scriptures.
    - You will encounter trials
    - Testing of your faith produces endurance
    - You can ask God for wisdom
    - We must ask God in faith
    - A double-minded man is unstable

 ## Homework Based On This Week's Lesson

- Create an individual plan and a plan as a couple to develop your personal intimacy with God

Homework In Preparation For The Next Lesson

- Each of you is to identify 2 people you need to establish healthy boundaries with. Then answer the question, if you established boundaries, what would be different in the relationship?

References

Marshall Segal, "Prayer for beginners," *Desiring God*, https://www.desiringgod.org/articles/prayer-for-beginners

Precept Austin, https://www.preceptaustin.org/

Robert Velarde, "Why Study the Bible?" *Focus on the Family*, https://www.focusonthefamily.com/faith/the-study-of-god/why-study-the-bible/why-study-the-bible

WEEK 6

Boundaries

Goals

- Review emotional and physical boundaries
- Discuss reasons people don't set boundaries
- Evaluate boundaries in life and consider boundaries to create
- Assess the need for boundaries in all relationships

Materials

- Pens

Advance Preparation

- None

Building Our Connection

As you are imagining the rest of your life, are there friendships that may need to end? Do you have a person you call your work wife or work husband? Is there someone in your life that knows more about your feelings than your future spouse? How much do your parents know about your relationship? In your future marriage, you will need people to talk to about your feelings and to help you address conflict in your marriage. However, you want to turn to people who are fighting for both of you and your marriage. Typically, your family members will not forgive your future spouse as quickly and easily as you. Therefore, you may need to find friends who are married to vent to, impartial people who will support and challenge you both to do better.

After the opening prayer, begin this week's group by reviewing the homework you completed.

This week's lesson will help you assess the need for appropriate boundaries individually and within your future family unit. The activities will explore physical and emotional boundaries.

Lesson Activities

Review the Rational Boundary-Building Thinking worksheet. Read through the worksheet, indicate which thoughts you relate to, discuss any unhealthy beliefs, and identify a boundary that could be created for the belief. Below are questions to ask:

- Which feelings clue you into the need to set a boundary?
- Which individuals are more difficult to set boundaries with?
- How do you think those individuals would respond to your boundaries?
- How would your life be improved with healthy boundaries?
- What surprised you in doing this activity?
- What was the most difficult part about this activity?
- What similarities did you notice between the areas where you need boundaries?

Personal Boundaries

Work through the Creating Personal Boundaries worksheet and discuss your response to the example given.

- Identify boundaries being violated in your life and create a plan to address the boundary violations.

Boundaries For Couples

Work through the Creating Boundaries as a Couple worksheet and discuss your response to the example given.

- Identify boundaries being violated and create a plan to address the boundary violations.

Homework Based On This Week's Lesson

- Continue discussing boundaries needed for your future marriage

Homework In Preparation For The Next Lesson

- Each person is to document the details of any disagreement you've had before working through the next lesson, include how the disagreement began, how it ended, who walked away, the feelings you experienced, tone of voice, body language, and the location of argument.

References

"Setting Healthy Boundaries," *Recovery Education Network*, http://www.recoveryeducationnetwork.org/uploads/9/6/6/3/96633012/boundary_setting_tips__1_.pdf

Rational Boundary & Building Thinking[5]

These are just a few examples of unhealthy thoughts or beliefs which allow boundaries to be ignored or violated. Following each unhealthy belief is a healthy, rational, realistic, reality-based affirmation for healthy boundary building.

Unhealthy Belief	Healthy Boundary Builder
I can never say "no" to others.	I have a right to say "no" to others if it is an invasion of my space or a violation of my rights.
It is my duty to hold them together.	I have a right to take care of myself. If they want to stay together as a family or group, it is up to each individual to make such a decision. We all share responsibility to create the interdependency needed to keep us a united group.
I can never trust anyone again.	I have a right to take the risk to grow in my relationships with others. If I find my rights are being violated or ignored, I can assertively protect myself to ensure I am not hurt.
I would feel guilty if I did something on my own and left my family or group out of it.	I have the right and need to do things which are uniquely mine so that I do not become so overly enmeshed with others that I lose my identity.
I should do everything I can to spend as much time together with you or else we won't be a healthy family or group.	I have a right and a need to explore my own interests, hobbies and outlets so that I can bring back to this family or group my unique personality to enrich our lives rather than be lost in a closed and over enmeshed system.
It doesn't matter what they are doing to me. As long as I keep quiet and don't complain, they will eventually leave me alone.	I will stand up for myself and assert my rights to be respected and not hurt or violated. If they choose to ignore me, then I have the right to leave them or ask them to get out of my life.
As long as I am not seen or heard, I won't be violated or hurt.	I have a right to be visible and to be seen and heard. I will stand up for myself so that others can learn to respect my rights, my needs and not violate my space.
I'd rather not pay attention to what is happening to me in this relationship which is overly intrusive, smothering and violating my privacy. In this way I don't have to feel the pain and hurt that comes from such a violation.	I choose no longer to disassociate from my feelings when I am being treated in a negatively and painful way so that I can be aware of what is happening to me and assertively protect myself from further violation or hurt.

---

[5] "Setting healthy Boundaries," *Recovery Education Network*, http://www.recoveryeducationnetwork.org/uploads/9/6/6/3/96633012/boundary_setting_tips__1_.pdf

Unhealthy Belief	Healthy Boundary Builder
I've been hurt badly in the past and I will never let anyone in close enough to hurt me again.	I do not need to be cold and distant or aloof and shy as protective tools to avoid being hurt. I choose to open myself up to others trusting that I will be assertive to protect my rights and privacy from being violated.
I can never tell where to draw the line with others.	There is a line I have drawn over which I do not allow others to cross. This line ensures me my uniqueness, autonomy and privacy. I am able to be me the way I really am rather than the way people want me to be by drawing this line. By this line I let others know: this is who I am and where I begin and you end; this is who you are and where you begin and I end; we will never cross over this line so that we can maintain a healthy relationship with one another.

Creating Personal Boundaries

The boundary being crossed is...	The action I will take is...
Example: My fiancé's uncle has made a habit of hitting me on my butt each time he sees me. His actions cause me to hate being around him.	I will discuss the inappropriate touching with my fiancé's uncle and let him know how it makes me feel. I will let him know that I will not allow him to touch me in the future.

Creating Boundaries as a Couple

The boundary being crossed is...	The action I will take is...
Example: My fiancé has an opposite sex coworker. They work late nights most days and talk and text throughout the day. They call each other work husband and work wife and kiss and hug each other when they meet and leave one another. I'm not comfortable with this behavior.	I plan to discuss boundaries with my fiancé and define clear boundaries for all opposite sex and same-sex relationships.

WEEK 7

Communication & Conflict

Goals

- Review Scripture about conflict, expressing anger, and forgiveness
- Develop ground rules for disagreements in relationships
- Practice using a conflict resolution model (decision making model)

Materials

- Bible or Bible app
- Pens
- Conflict resolution model worksheet

Advance Preparation

- None

Building Our Connection

In the beginning of your relationship, talking was easy. You and your future spouse talked for hours about almost any subject that was presented. However, as time went on, you both learned there were topics that elicited strong emotions so you made mental notes to avoid those topics. Other topics perhaps added to your "list to work on" so you avoided those as well.

There are a number or reasons why conversations don't go well. Sometimes, couples attempt to have conversations while distracted so you rarely hear everything that is being said. Whether there is noise going on around you, be it other people around, the television, the use of cell phones or the story constantly playing in your head; to do anything undistracted anymore is rare. How many times have you seen couples sitting in a restaurant and one or both parties is doing something on their phone while barely talking with the person across from them?

In a time when busy is a badge of honor and technology has completely taken over, it is difficult to stay present in the moment. Couples don't always set the stage to have a conversation before speaking. Having disagreements isn't a sign of an unhealthy relationship. It could be a sign of the wrong time or envioronment for a serious conversation. Additionally, it is a way of expressing an unmet need or unspoken expectations. Disagreements will happen and in order to prepare for them set ground rules. Here are a few tips to create an environment conducive for conversations. First, commit to talking at a specific time and when you both are rested and eager to bring the conversation to a conclusion peacefully. Secondly, reduce environmental distractions so your discussion can be fruitful. This could include silencing your cell phones, turning off the television, and helping the children occupy their time apart from you. Lastly, determine the topic to discuss. As a couple, agree to discuss one topic and set a date and time to revisit any other topics.

After the opening prayer, begin this week's lesson by reviewing the boundaries you identified for your future marriage. Below are questions to ask:

- What was most revealing about this activity?
- What are the boundaries you cannot agree to implement?
- What is a boundary you're struggling to implement?

This week's activities will encourage you to communicate more deeply and provide practical ways to resolve differences. The activities will provide you insight into areas where you may need help with constructive ways to tackle issues and help learning to listen.

Lesson Activities

Review and discuss Scriptures on communication and conflict.

Read Psalms 15:1–3, Psalms 37:7–9, Psalms 141:3–4, Proverbs 12:15–19, Proverbs 29:11, Ecclesiastes 7:9, Matthew 15:18–19, Ephesians 4:25–27, Ephesians 4:29–32, and James 1:19–20.

Below are questions to ask:

- How was anger expressed in your childhood home?
- When is anger wrong?
- How do you respond when you're angry? How do you respond to other people's anger?
- You've heard people say they don't want to go to bed angry. What are your thoughts?

Conflict Resolution Activity

A Conflict Resolution Model provides a method to discuss and resolve differences in opinions and preferences. Work through the Conflict Resolution Model worksheet using an issue you have not resolved. It is highly encouraged that you come up with 10 possible solutions. Usually the last few solutions are the best options to resolve the issue.

Just Listen

In this activity, one person talks about anything they want for 4 minutes without the other person interrupting. After the timer ends, the listening partner recaps the discussion. Next, the other person talks for 4 minutes without interruption. After the timer ends, the listening partner recaps the discussion. After each person has spoken and recapped the talking points, ask questions to learn more about your future spouse. Setting a timer is helpful with this activity.

Fight Fair

In this activity, you will work on creating a list of 5-10 ground rules to minimize the impact of disagreements on your future marriage. Some ground rule examples are:
- We will not refer to each other using derogatory words.
- We will not use foul language.

After you've identified your ground rules, review the questions below:
- When will you discuss disagreements? At the time of the offense or after a cooling off period?
- How will you respond if one person needs a timeout and the other person prefers to attempt to resolve the argument quickly?
- How long are the timeouts? Who re-engages after a timeout is taken?
- If you're unable to resolve a conflict, when will you bring others into your disagreement?

Homework Based On This Week's Lesson

- Complete the Apology Assessment, https://www.5lovelanguages.com/profile/apology/ and discuss the results with your significant other.
- Continue setting aside 15-minutes, 3 times a week to talk and preparing for the upcoming week.

Homework In Preparation For The Next Lesson

- As a couple, identify those individuals and couples, who currently make up your community and discuss ways your community can be more supportive.

References

"Conflict Resolutions Model," *Prepare Enrich*, https://www.prepare-enrich.com/

Gary Chapman, "The Apology Languages," *The 5 Love Languages*, https://www.5lovelanguages.com/profile/apology/

Conflict Resolution Model

What is the topic to be discussed?	
His Response	Her Response

What is a good time and place to discuss the topic?	
His Response	Her Response

How do you and your future spouse view the topic?	
His Response	Her Response

How have you and your future spouse tried to address the topic in the past?	
His Response	Her Response

What are 10 possible solutions? REQUIRED!

1.		6.	
2.		7.	
3.		8.	
4.		9.	
5.		10.	

How will each of you work towards executing the selected decision?	
His Response	Her Response

What is a good time and place to meet to evaluate our progress?	
His Response	Her Response

The Road To We

WEEK 8

Building Community

Goals

- Review God's purpose of community and the benefits of community
- Explore when to engage mentors and community
- Define characteristics of healthy and unhealthy mentors
- Consider marriage without the benefit of community

Materials

- Bible or Bible app
- Pens

Advance Preparation

- None

Building Our Connection

In order to have a healthy relationship, it is paramount that you build community by making a commitment to surround yourselves with healthy couples. In addition, to have a healthy relationship, you must get comfortable with letting people in your business. Of course, use discernment when deciding who to let in and at what level. Make sure those you let in have a healthy relationship with God, are providing biblically based guidance, and have your best interest in mind whether you like what they may say or not.

After the opening prayer, begin this week's lesson by checking in on the homework from the previous lesson. Below are questions to ask:

- Were you able to identify a solution to the issue you discussed that is acceptable to both of you?
- How will you begin using the Apology Assessment results to resolve disagreements?

This week's lesson will focus on God's will for individuals and couples to live in community. Initially, the lesson will focus on developing friends and will end with living in community and joining life groups. This week's activities will guide you in evaluating your personal reasons for keeping people at a distance, living in isolation, having few or no friends, or not trusting people.

Lesson Activities

Begin by discussing your childhood and history as it relates to having friends and being a friend.

- Did you grow up in a home where you were told "don't tell anybody our business?" How did this impact your relationships as a child and as an adult?
- How can living by this statement positively and negatively impact your future marriage?
- Do you have friends that you talk to that your future spouse trusts?
- As a woman, have you ever said, "I don't have a lot of female friends because I don't trust women?"
    - If so, why don't you trust women?
- As a man, have you ever said, "I don't have a lot of male friends, I stick to myself."
    - If so, why don't you trust men?
- Why do you prefer to live with few friends or off to yourself?
- Do you want a couple of "good" friends?
- Have you ever hurt a friend and regretted the situation? What happened?
    - What would you do differently if you could?
    - How has that event and loss of that friendship shaped you?
- How do you make friends as adults?
    - Cultivate an acquaintance (nurture this relationship and with time it will either grow or dissolve)
    - Meet new people doing activities you enjoy (church, playing sports, volunteering

Scripture

Review and discuss Scriptures on God's design for living life in community.

Read Psalms 1:1, Proverbs 1:5, Proverbs 19:20–21, Proverbs 12:15, Proverbs 20:18, Proverbs 11:14, and Proverbs 24:5–6.

Below are some questions to ask:

- According to the Bible, what are some advantages of seeking advice from others?
- What could be some disadvantages of seeking advice from others?
- What are some characteristics of people who are safe to consider developing friendships with?
- What are some characteristics of people who are unsafe to develop friendships with?
- How do you know if you're a good judge of character?
- What are some reasons people isolate themselves and don't live in community?
    - Fear of being gossiped about
    - Fear of being hurt
    - Fear of being taken advantage of
    - Fear of being rejected
    - Personal insecurities (I'm not funny enough, I don't have anything to talk about, no one wants to hang out with me, etc.)
- Do any of those fears keep you from developing new relationships or joining a community?
- Do you have other married or engaged friends that you and your future spouse can hang out with?
- Identify 2-3 married mentor couples that can walk alongside you and your future spouse.
    - Discuss with your significant other whether or not the mentor couple you're considering is healthy or unhealthy and why?

- What are some characteristics of safe couples?
    - Have a personal relationship with Jesus Christ.
    - Willing to share what God has done in and through their marriage.
    - Have a growing marriage of at least 5 years, understanding that it is not perfect but they are striving for a healthy marriage.
- When would you bring the mentors, married couples, or life group community into your decision-making process or disagreements with your spouse?
- Can your single friends be mentors to you as a married couple?
- What role should your single friends have in your life as a married couple?

 **Homework Based On This Week's Lesson**

- Contact one of the possible mentor couples and meet with them as a couple (date night).

Homework In Preparation For The Next Lesson

- Create a budget for the next lesson. Find a budget format online.

The Road To We

WEEK 9

Money Is A Tool

Goals

- Review God's design and plan for money
- Discuss how to handle debt, giving, and saving
- Evaluate the advantages and disadvantages of family business meetings

Materials

- Bible or Bible app
- Marriage Roadmap
- Pens or markers
- Debt List worksheet
- Idea List worksheet
- Calendars (any medium)

Advance Preparation

- None

Building Our Connection

Research states that four out of five Americans use a budget to plan their monthly spending and 20 percent of them keep only a mental budget. Simply putting your budget on paper or in a fancy budgeting spreadsheet, if that suits you, is essential if you want a healthy financial future. Creating a detailed budget is key to managing your finances. By sticking to a budget, you can save lots of money over time and avoid overspending and many days and nights arguing with your future spouse over money.

It may sound complicated, but budgeting can actually be a very basic personal finance skill. Whether you decide to make your budget very simple or so detailed that you zero out the last dollar, the most important part of budgeting is to put it into practice and tracking your spending is essential to managing your budget. Your budget should be reviewed regularly and adjustments made accordingly.

You and your future spouse will determine who will manage the finances and the way those finances are managed. Since the beginning of time, bringing two people together in any capacity has never been characterized as simplistic. Depending on what you've observed from your future spouse, you may be hesitant to allow them to manage the finances in marriage. Perhaps you've seen careless spending, inconsiderate purchases or even unauthorized loans. If so, discuss these situations with your future spouse. If money is a difficult topic to discuss, 1) write down your thoughts and feelings, 2) plan a time to discuss your concerns with your future spouse, and 3) stick to the agreed upon date and time, and 4) tackle the subject. If you cannot discuss money before marriage, it will not be an easier conversation after marriage. Seek help from mentors as needed.

This week's group will focus on God's design and His plan for money. As a couple, you will evaluate your debt and devise ways to positively impact your budgets.

Lesson Activities

Review and discuss Scriptures related to ownership, stewardship, debt, giving, and saving.

Ownership vs. Stewardship

Read Leviticus 25:23, 1 Corinthians 10:26, 1 Corinthians 4:2, Luke 16:1–2, Philippians 4:19, and Matthew 6:30–34.

- What does God own?

- What do you own?

- How are stewards to conduct themselves?

- God has promised to meet your needs (Phil 4:19). Why do you struggle believing this statement?

- What are some of your motivations behind gambling, betting or playing the lottery?

- How does God view gambling, betting or playing the lottery?

Debt
Read Proverbs 22:7 and Psalms 37:21.

- Why is debt discouraged?
- What is your plan to get out of debt?
- As a couple how will you handle each other's debts?
- When should you co-sign for others?

Giving
Read Proverbs 3:27–28 and Malachi 3:8–10.

- What are your thoughts about giving to God or others?
- What is the impact of not giving to God or others?
- What is your plan to increase your giving to God and others?

Saving
Read 1 Timothy 5:8, Genesis 41:34–36, 1 Timothy 6:9–10, and Proverbs 27:23–24.

- How was money handled in your childhood home?
- How did you learn about managing money?
- Why should you save for the future?
- If you don't save and are able to save, why don't you save?
- If you do save, what are your savings goals beyond your wedding?

Identify Your Debt

- Using the Debt List worksheet, as a couple create a list of the debts you both have as of today. Of those debts listed, indicate which debts you will pay off before marriage.
- Using the Ideas to Reduce Debt worksheet, as a couple identify any ideas you could implement to decrease debt and expenses or to increase income.
- As a couple, develop a detailed plan to pay off at least 2 debts and add the milestones to your Marriage Roadmap.
- For debt-free couples, create financial goals and add the milestones to your Marriage Roadmap.
  - For example, a goal could be to save 1 year's salary. You would add a quarterly or semi-annual milestone representing the amount you should have saved by that milestone.

Family Meeting

With busy lifestyles, it is important to set aside time to review your progress towards your goals. One way to achieve this goal is to have a monthly family meeting. Just as businesses have meetings, having a family meeting will help you both align your understanding of your progress. In future meetings, including the children, teaches them the value of planning and budgeting and working as a team. Discuss the purpose and the benefits for family business meetings. Plan your first family business meeting to occur one month after your wedding. In the planning, include a high-level agenda, frequency, and attendance requirement (for those with older children).

- As a couple discuss the concept of an annual family meeting and ways you could implement the activity into your new union.

 ## Homework Based On This Week's Lesson

- Conduct a spending plan analysis based on your proposed budget. Using your joint budget, calculate the percentage of your income spent in various categories and compare the percentages with the recommended percentages. Search the internet for Personal Budget Percentages. While the percentages vary based on each couples' unique circumstances, evaluate any outliers for potential problems.

Homework In Preparation For The Next Lesson

- Individually identify obstacles that could interfere with dating, intimate time spent together, and sexual intimacy in marriage. Also, identify ways you can proactively prepare for those identified obstacles.

Premarital Couples Workbook

Our Debt List

Who do you owe money to?	What type of debt is it?	How much do you owe?	What is your monthly payment?	Monthly due date	Projected payoff date
Nordstrom	Credit Card	$1,250	$75	15th	4/12/2021
Sallie Mae	Student Loan	$56,743	$421.15	3rd	12/20/2045

Ideas To Reduce Debt

Idea	Will this increase income or decrease expenses?	How to execute your plan?
Sell unwanted or duplicate household items		Hold a garage sale before the wedding
Get a second job		Offer freelance services online Join a focus group service
Eat out less frequently		Cook dinner and make lunch at home during the week

WEEK 10

Intimacy

Goals

- Review God's design for intimacy
- Contrast the world's view of intimacy
- Explore ways to grow in intimacy
- Develop boundaries in intimacy

Materials

- None

Advance Preparation

- None

Building Our Connection

Many people have had a few sexual experiences with their future spouse or others. As a result, discussing sex proves challenging because people who are sexually active don't want to stop engaging in sex. The media portrays a single person's sexual escapades as magical, passionate, spontaneous, life-giving, and toe-curling. A single person can have sex any time, any place, with any available person without regard for commitment or consequences. Conversely, the media stereotypically characterizes marital intimacy as drudgery, monotonous, and lifeless. Something to do with your spouse, every year on their birthday or yours, until you die. However, when God created Adam and Eve in the Genesis narrative, He said, "It was very good." (Gen 1:30) God created Adam and Eve for their mutual enjoyment (Gen 2:18, 20, 24) and procreation (Gen 1:28).

Often couples desire to live together to evaluate their ability to exist day and night together. One study suggested, "…experience may provide benefit in some realms, like employment, but not in the case of marital quality."[6] Couples living together before marriage must contend with managing a temporary dating relationship while living as though they're married. Dating relationships have enough pressure, don't intensify the strain by "playing

---

[6] http://www.deseretnews.com/article/865609072/How-a-persons-premarital-experiences-affect-his-or-her-future-marriage.html

house." Give the relationship time to develop and grow. Give yourself the freedom to move towards marriage or to end the relationship without the added stress of living together.

Keep in mind if you or your future spouse have been sexually abused or sexually assaulted, abuse trauma can impact behaviors, thinking, and relationships. The trauma can negatively affect a person's feelings about intimacy, romantic affection, and sexual boundaries. It is unwise to consider marrying a person who you think can fix the hurt of your abuse. Your future spouse was not meant to heal you; only God can heal you. Therefore, turn to God to help heal old hurts and pain. Additionally, seek help from a pastoral counselor or a licensed professional counselor before getting married. This can be a healing time for both you and your future spouse.

After opening prayer, begin this week's lesson by reviewing the finance homework. Below are some questions to ask each other:

- What did you learn about your spending habits when comparing your percentages to the average percentages?
- What are some habits that you may need to change to bring your spending under control?
- What is the most "questionable" thing you have purchased on credit?
- What are some things you could sell to help improve your current financial situation?

This week's lesson will examine emotional and physical intimacy in marriage and will conclude the journey with a recap of the weekly lessons.

Lesson Activities

Discuss self-care as a couple.

- What is self-care? What isn't self-care?
    - Some answers are not caring for yourself mentally, physically, and emotionally, being overly critical, infidelity, not having any friends outside of the relationship, not apologizing, etc.
- What are activities that re-energize you that you enjoy doing with anyone other than your significant other?
    - When is the last time you enjoyed any of those activities?
    - If it has been a while, why haven't you taken time away from your significant

other?
- How can participating in those activities that you enjoy away from your significant other help your future marriage?
- If you don't know what you enjoy, how can you identify activities you enjoy?
  - Consider things you did before you started dating your significant other
  - Assess activities you wish you could do but never made time to learn them
  - Listen to things other people do and to see if you'd enjoy them
  - Try physical activities like gym classes, yoga, or exercising
  - Try activities like reading, meditating, or attending a conference on a topic you enjoy learning about
  - Try spiritual activities like conducting an in-depth Bible study on a specific topic, or a particular book of the bible, attending a Christian concert, conference, or watching a sermon of a pastor different than your own pastor who is biblically-based.

- How do you think caring for yourself will help your future marriage?
- How do you think caring for yourself can hurt your future marriage?
- How is your mental health?
  - Are there areas or issues you need to address before marriage?
  - What are the childhood issues you have not addressed?
  - Do you need to seek the services of a licensed counselor?
  - What are some things that can negatively impact your intimacy with your spouse?

The World's View Of Sex

This discussion will explore society's teaching on emotional and physical intimacy as singles and married couples. Below are some questions to ask:

- What is society's definition of intimacy?
- How does your definition differ?
- How does society encourage people to grow in intimacy?
- How do you think you can grow in non-physical intimacy with your spouse once married?

Scripture

Review and discuss Scriptures on God's design for sexual intimacy.

Read Genesis 1:27–31, 1 Corinthians 7:1-5, 1 Corinthians 7:8–9, and 1 Thessalonians 4:3–5.

Below are questions to ask:

- What do these verses tell you about God's design for man and woman?
- What do these verses tell you about seeking to have your own sexual desires fulfilled?
- How can self-seeking pleasure impact your marriage?
- How does the Bible view living together before marriage if you don't have sex?
- Can you stop having sex until you get married, even if you are living together? If not, why?
- Who in your life will help hold you accountable for purity until marriage?
- What is the impact of unaddressed sexual abuse or rape on a marriage?
- What is the impact of watching pornography on a marriage?
- What is the impact of unaddressed medical or mental health issue on a marriage?
- Why is God bringing you two together?
- What are ways you can work on increasing intimacy in other areas of your relationship (emotional intimacy, spiritual intimacy, recreational intimacy, intellectual intimacy)?
- What boundaries are needed in emotional intimacy with your significant other?
    - Some examples include each individual is responsible for their own emotions and mental health, their own health, their own relationship with God, to control their own body, has their own preferences, opinions, and beliefs, and can say no.
- What boundaries are needed in emotional intimacy with other people?
    - Some examples include limiting time spent alone with certain friends, minimizing communications with certain friends your significant other doesn't trust, or restraining the desire to share relationship issues with other people excluding mentors or life group members.

- How can you prioritize your marriage in all your interactions with friends?
  - Can either of you talk to opposite sex people on the phone, text, social media, etc.?
  - Can either of you talk to opposite sex people you've had sex with on the phone, text, social media, etc.?
- What boundaries are needed in regards to sexual intimacy before marriage?
  - Some examples include minimizing time alone, prohibiting touching and fondling of breasts, stomach, or genitals, reducing seductive and sexually stimulating conversations, or waiting to be sexually intimate until marriage.
- What boundaries are need in sexual intimacy in marriage?
  - Some examples include being able to say no, having sexual preferences and dislikes different from your spouse, or minimizing the tendency to use sex as a reward or punishment.

People have repeatedly said, sex starts outside of the bedroom. What does this statement mean? Do you believe this statement? If everyone believes this statement, why don't couples put more effort into building a connection and intimacy outside of the bedroom?

Book Recap

Below is a recap of the lessons you reviewed with your future spouse. The activities in this workbook were meant to bring you closer by building a deeper connection beyond simple head knowledge.

You discussed conflict, communication, and had regular homework on communication.
- How difficult has it been to spend 15-minutes talking 3 times a week?
- How will you work towards incorporating this activity into your lives?

You defined Roles, Expectations, and Boundaries.
- How have you been serving your significant other based on their love languages?
- How have you been working on changes to improve the interactions with your significant other?

- What boundaries have you established?
- How have those new boundaries impacted your relationships?

You discussed healing past hurts.
- Have you forgiven the person or people you mentioned during that lesson?
- Have you gotten professional help to work through the issues?

You discussed intimacy with God.
- Discuss the time you're spending with God and in His word.
- What is your established rhythm for reading God's word and praying?
- If you still haven't developed a rhythm, what is holding you back? What are you afraid of?

You discussed finances and plotted the marriage roadmap.
- What aspects of financial management are you still struggling to learn? How will you learn about that aspect of budgeting?
- How are you tracking to meet the financial goals you set?

You discussed community.
- Have you joined a married life group?
- How are the interactions between you and the other couples in your new group?
- Do you think the life group is a good fit?
- What are you learning about yourself as you get acquainted with the new group?

**YOU DID IT! You and your future spouse walked through hours of discussions preparing for marriage.
Praise God for your diligence, patience, and willingness to plan for a marriage to last a lifetime!**

Our Prayer for You

Future Husband

We pray that you heal from your past hurts and walk into the role God has called you to fulfill. We pray that you learn that in God's eyes you are wanted, loved, and not a mistake. We pray that you learn to lead from the front and not from the back. We pray you learn about your wife as a friend, a woman, and as a mother.

Future Wife

We pray that you allow yourself to be vulnerable with others who are safe. We pray that God teaches you to forgive quickly and to fear no one but Him. We pray that you learn to allow your husband to lead you even when he makes mistakes. We pray that you offer yourself to him without reservation.

Future Couple

We pray that you open yourselves up to meet new people and to extend yourselves in community. We pray that you stay connected to a life group, that can offer support, encouragement, and help nurture and guide your union. We pray that you set aside your pride and ask for help before any situation becomes a crisis.

In Jesus' Name. Amen.

Love,
The Relationship Roadwork Team

Thank you for taking part in our mission to build healthy relationships for a lifetime.™

About the Authors

The Road to We: Premarital Couples Workbook was written by a trio of married, professional Christian women with influence and guidance from their husbands, all who have a heart for walking with singles that desire to marry one day. With over 45 years of marital experience between them, these women know the importance of praying through all seasons of life.

Other books by

PRE-MARITAL PRAYER BOOKS

Prays for Me, Before We - A Wife in the Making

Prayers for Me, Before Me - A Husband in the Making

PRE-MARITAL CURRICULUM

The Road to We - Small Group Leader's Guide

Available everywhere books are sold.

Connect with Authors

Learn more about Road to We at www.relationshiproadwork.com
Share reflections and questions by emailing info@relationshiproadwork.com or social media using @rel8nshproadwrk.

Mail correspondences to
Relationship Road Work, LLC
PO Box 142621
Irving, TX 75014

www.ingramcontent.com/pod-product-compliance
Lightning Source LLC
Chambersburg PA
CBHW081755100526
44592CB00015B/2444